MOODS AND MOMENTS

MOODS
and
MOMENTS

By
LINDLEY J. STILES

WITH ASSISTANCE FROM
MARGUERITE, JUDITH AND PATRICIA

Original copyright, 1955, by the AuthorPublished by Garrett and Massey, Richmond, Virginia
Illustrations in original book by Sally Sargent Turner. Original Designer of Moods and Moments, Charles W. Smith Artist for Ideas and Images, from which "All most full grown" section is taken was Clarice Logan, Designed by Fred George Logan. Colored cover of new book is by artist Lori Musil. Design is by Simrnie G. Plummer

Printed and distributed for:
THE BEST SHOULD TEACH INITIATIVES,
At theTHE UNIVERSITY OF COLORADO AT BOULDER
And FORT LEWIS COLLEGE IN DURANGO, COLORADO

National Library of Canada Cataloguing in Publication Data
Stiles, J. Lindley
Moods and moments : in rhymes and rythms for children and youths
J. Lindley Stiles.
ISBN 1-4120-0882-4
I. Title.
PZ7.S8564Mo 2004 j811'.6 C2003-904262-6

TRAFFORD

This book was published *on-demand* in cooperation with Trafford Publishing.
On-demand publishing is a unique process and service of making a book available for retail
sale to the public taking advantage of on-demand manufacturing and Internet marketing.
On-demand publishing includes promotions, retail sales, manufacturing, order fulfilment, accounting and collecting royalties on behalf of the author.

Suite 6E, 2333 Government St., Victoria, B.C. V8T 4P4, CANADA
Phone 250-383-6864 Toll-free 1-888-232-4444 (Canada & US)
Fax 250-383-6804 E-mail sales@trafford.com
Web site www.trafford.com
TRAFFORD PUBLISHING IS A DIVISION OF TRAFFORD HOLDINGS LTD.
Trafford Catalogue #03-1250 www.trafford.com/robots/03-1250.html

10 9 8 7 6 5 4 3 2

FOREWORD—A BOOK LIVES ON

Moods and Moments is as re-print of a classic collection of poems for children and young people that deal with their experiences while growing up in an American home. Originally published in 1955, it was judged the equal to the poems of the famous English poet, A. A. Milne. It was a best seller of poetry books in its time. Poems such as "The Top Drawer," "Can God See Me," "My Favorite Queen," "What's Your Name," and "A Mother's Regret," have been included in various anthologies of children's literature over the years. The book itself, has been sold and re-sold on the used book market in book stores and on the internet. By popular demand, it is now being released by Trafford Printing to support efforts to strengthen family living throughout the world.

It is popular poetry for children and young people as well as parents and teachers.. Its sparkling rhymes and rhythms as well as its delightful illustrations reveal with delicate sensitivity events that most children experience as they are growing up. Written about the life of one family, readers have attested that it belongs to all. From the early childhood experience of 'Johnny One Hop", through the through the wonderful reflections of "Turn Loose My Hand", to the galloping, saddle-back rhythms of "Round-up Time," no reader,young or old, will be untouched.

In-store for all who read these verses will be wit and wisdom, wonder and relaxation, recalled personal memories, as well as tears and laughter found in wholesome family living. It is a book that, once started, is difficult to put down—in the initial and subsequent readings. And, through it the reader will find communion with a Who's Who poet who has been named by the International Biographical Centre, in Cambridge, England as "One of a few Greatest Living Legends."

Boulder, Colorado
Dr. Lindley J. Stiles

CONTENTS

EARLY YEARS

The Only Boy 3
Johnny One-Hop—The Two Finger Man 4
Nothing to Fear 5
Can God See Me? 6
The Top Drawer 7
Why? 9
A Race 9
Buy Me Something 10
Accomplishments-Age Three 11
On Top 12
Let Me See 13
God Heard Our Prayer 14
What is a Dream? 15
My Friend Teddy 17
The Clock's Face 19

CONTENTS

A LITTLE LATER

Growing 23
A Little Conscience 23
Take Me to the Pet Shop 24
Tum Loose My Hand 26
In a Minute 27
What Do You Say? 28
My Favorite Queen 29
What's Your Name? 30
My Hide-Away 33
The Ocean Waves 35
Disappointment 36
Big Sister's Room 37
Someone to Walk for Me 39

CONTENTS

IN-BETWEEN YEARS

In-Between 43
Parents 43
Center of Attention 44
Slumber Party 45
How Will I Look? 46
Who, Me? 48
Bargaining 49
The Cover-Up 50
Family Decisions 50
Teen-Age Friends 51
In Style 52
"The" Night 54
Lost Vacation 55
Oldern Times 57
A Mother's Regret 58
Hold the Phone 59
A Plea to Fathers of Sons 60
For A Happy Family 61

CONTENTS

ALMOST FULL GROWN

Assessment 65
Belonging 66
Travel Guide 67
Priorities 68
Feed Back 69
Empathy 69
Curiosity 70
Obsolete 71
Vanity 71
Hate 72
Doubt 72
Dawn or Dusk 73
Left Out 74
Seasoning 75
Secrets 78
Youth and Age 79
Round-up Time 80
Immortality 89

A Dedicated Book 90
About The Author 92

CONTENTS

ALMOST FULL GROWN

Assessment 65
Belonging 66
Travel Guide 67
Priorities 68
Feed Back 69
Empathy 69
Curiosity 70
Obsolete 71
Vanity 71
Hate 72
Doubt 72
Dawn or Dusk 73
Left Out 74
Seasoning 75
Secrets 78
Youth and Age 79
Round-up Time 80
Immortality 89

A Dedicated Book 90
About The Author 92

EARLY YEARS

Quickly passed, long remembered.

THE ONLY BOY

Mommy is a girl; Sister's a girl,
    The third girl, you can guess who;
Daddy's the only boy at our house,
    Our puppy's a girl, too.

JOHNNY ONE-HOP—THE TWO FINGER MAN

Johnny One-Hop is a funny little man,
  Made of two fingers of Daddy's big hand;
One leg is short, the other is quite long—
  He walks with a hop, and is very strong.

When lying in bed, right flat of my back,
  I feel on my tummy his wobbly track;
He steps on my ribs and slides all around,
  Then he jumps on my head with a great big bound.

Across my two lips he walks with great care,
  Then shuffles his feet all through my blond hair;
If I don't shut my eyes he'll step into them,
  He hops on my ear and skips round the rim.

Along my wee nose he climbs to the point,
  Runs round my chin 'til my jaw's out-of-joint,
From laughing and shouting and nudging this man
  Who's made of two fingers of Daddy's big hand.

NOTHING TO FEAR

Wind, rain and thunder,
    Lightning strikes a tree;
What is there to fear,
    With Mother near me?

CAN GOD SEE ME?

In church, I'm too small to see around
 The fancy hats and the men who frown;
I see the prayer book in the rack,
 And pretty lace on a lady's back.

I can hear the organ as it plays,
 And the minister's voice whenever he prays;
I see the top of a window bright,
 And a tall candle with its tiny light.

I see the cross when I stand tiptoe,
 It's high on the wall where it will show;
If God's up front, I cannot see—
 I often wonder, can God see me?

THE TOP DRAWER

Of all the things
    I'd like to know,
About the wonders
    That trouble me so,
One question comes
    And will not stop:
What is in that
    Drawer on top?

Mother puts in
    Then takes things out;
Daddy fumbles
    And looks about;
It must be deep
    And hold a lot!
This mysterious
    Drawer on top.

To be so small,
    Not able to see,
Is the very biggest
    Problem to me.
I want to grow,
    And never stop—
Until I reach that
    Drawer on top.

WHY?

Oh, why am I?
    And why are you?
Why is this so,
    And that untrue?

Why is the morning?
    And why is the night?
Why does the sun shine,
    And the moon give light?

Why is grass short?
    Why are trees tall?
Why did God make
    The world at all?

Why must I come?
    Why can't I go?
Why everything—
    I'd like to know?

A RACE

Very soon after she starts to walk,
    A little girl begins to talk;
And the race is never quite complete
    Between her tongue and her bouncing feet.

BUY ME SOMETHING

Buy me something, Daddy,
  While you are in town;
A brand new rubber dolly,
  A ball that's big and round.

Buy me something, won't you?
  While you are away;
A book with pretty pictures,
  Or a game that I can play.

Buy me something always,
  These words ring in my ear.
'Til I return to proudly say,
  "Look what I've bought you, dear."

ACCOMPLISHMENTS — AGE THREE

I can run and hop and jump;
I can skip, see me!
I can swing by just my toes;
I am only three.

ON TOP

Wherever I am
    I never stop,
Trying to climb
    To get on top.

On top the bed,
    On top the chair;
I cannot wait
    To see what's there.

I'm never happy
    Unless I try
To reach the top,
    No matter how high.

When I grow up,
    Will I ever stop,
Or still keep trying
    To climb on top?

LET ME SEE

Won't someone lift me up and let me see
    What's on the table and the Christmas Tree,
What is in that bowl on top of the shelf;
    I'm not tall enough to see by myself.

GOD HEARD OUR PRAYER

When Mother was sick,
  We sent a prayer;
To ask help from God
  Who lives way up there.

I was not so sure
  It would reach His home;
With no radio,
  And no telephone.

God heard our prayer,
  For Mother got well;
That is one sure way
  We can always tell.

WHAT IS A DREAM?

An ugly animal tried to eat me,
I was as scared as scared could be;
I pulled at my pillow and loudly screamed,
My mother said, "Honey, you must have dreamed."

Just what is a dream, I would like to know?
When all is quiet and lights are low,
Things frighten me, then I wake up weeping,
Mother tucks me in and sighs, "You're sleeping."

So many things happen to me in sleep
    I would like to tell, but I dare not peep;
Daddy says, "Things are not as they seem,
    What to you is real, is only a dream."

Do big folks dream as does a little tyke,
    About strange places and the things they like?
What is a dream, if it is not true?
    They seem real to me; do they to you?

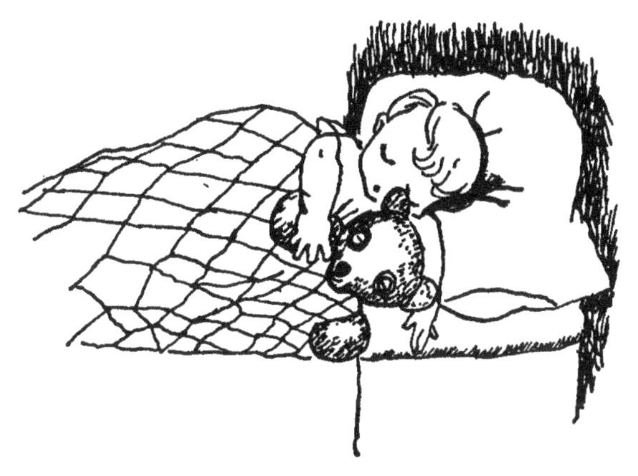

MY FRIEND TEDDY

I've a little Teddy,
With fur so soft and brown;
He has a stubby tail,
And black eyes big and round.

He goes to bed with me,
Where'er I am each night;
I hold him very close,
Then I can sleep real tight.

And when I am lonely
'Cause Mother is not there,
It makes me feel better
To hug my Teddy Bear.

Teddy's like a dear friend,
    One always wants real near;
He shares all my troubles,
    And helps me see things clear.

I am so very sorry
    For others who have cares,
Who need close friends beside them,
    And have no Teddy Bears.

THE CLOCK'S FACE

Sometimes the clock wears a great big smile,
But often its mouth is closed tight;
And then its head seems tilted sideways
When we're ready for dinner each night.

The clock can frown and twist its mouth
To suit just the way it feels;
Whenever it pouts, if you'll wait long enough
It'll change to a smile that appeals.

In mornings and evenings, the clock
Always holds its mouth the same way;
By watching its face we learn to know
How 'twill look any time of day.

A LITTLE LATER

A spirited race with the children often in front!

GROWING

I'm now tall enough
    To reach across the bed;
I put my toes on one side,
    On the other is my head.

A LITTLE CONSCIENCE

When I am bad
    I'm sure that I
Will never go to heaven.

But, really I
    Don't worry much,
For I am only seven.

TAKE ME TO THE PET SHOP

Take me to the pet shop, I'd like to go
    Get me a little mouse as white as snow;
To play with and love, a pet of my own
    To live with our family right in our home.

But Daddy always looks far ahead
    He must not like pets, for here's what he said;
He reasoned as follows about what I asked—
    What seemed a small thing, he made quite a task.

If we get a mouse
    Then we'd need a cat,
To catch the mouse or
    It would be a rat;
To catch the cat we
    Would need a big dog,
Or else the old cat
    Might hide in a log;
To control the dog
    A lion we'd need;
To no smaller animals
    Dogs will pay heed;
Who'd manage the lion
    I now hear you chant,
For that job we'd need
    A big elephant!

A mouse, cat, dog, lion and big elephant,
    Are so many pets that Daddy just can't
Find room to keep them with us in our house—
    But all I wanted was one tiny mouse!

TURN LOOSE MY HAND

We walked along, both hand in hand,
    Across the street toward a brand new land;
According to custom and the rule,
    I was taking our first to school.

'Twas then I heard a whisper clear,
    "Turn loose my hand, please Mother dear;
For I won't need you anymore—
    There is my teacher at the door."

IN A MINUTE

When Mother calls Daddy
    Both loudly and clear,
He most always replies,
    "In a minute, my dear."

And big Sister, also,
    Who should come on the run;
Answers Mother smugly,
    "In a minute, I'll come."

No matter the reason,
    Or how great Mother's need,
Both Daddy and Sister
    Seem to pay little heed.

Mother's always patient
    With these people of ours;
She knows, "In a minute,"
    May well stretch into hours.

But when Mother calls me,
    With, "It's bedtime for you,"
And I try the same trick
    Of "In a minute," too,

She is patient no longer
    A frown crosses her brow;
She looks at me sternly,
    Saying, "You'll come right now."

WHAT DO YOU SAY?

What do you say to the lady
    Who gives you a piece of candy?
"Thank you, Mam, thank you very much,"
    Now isn't that just dandy!
"What do you say," spoils all good things,
    A game, someone gives me to play,
I'm grateful and happy—but then
    Mother ruins it with "What do you say?"

MY FAVORITE QUEEN

Of all the queens that I have known,
  In real life, fairy tale, or fancy grown;
Like Queen Victoria or Good Queen Bess,
  Yes, the Queen of Hearts and all the rest;
The Gypsy Queen, the Queen of the Ball—
  Add the Queen of Sheba, among them all—
Queens with beauty, grandeur and power,
  Wearing splendid costumes every hour;
For every occasion beautiful gowns,
  Ornate headdresses with jeweled crowns—
But my favorite queen, wherever we stop,
  Is the *Dairy Queen with the Curl on Top.*

WHAT'S YOUR NAME?

How old are you,
    And what's your name?
Was ever a child
    Who missed this game?
No matter who asks,
    The question's the same:
How old are you,
    What is your name?

What a sweet child,
    How old are you?
So big and strong—
    You're only two!
And what's your name?
    Oh, let me guess:
Is it Sue, Pat,
    Helen or Bess?

How you have grown!
    How old, let's see?
(Can't she tell
    I'm now past three).
Your name again,
    Do let me hear?
(The answer's simple—
    Same as last year).

This was your baby;
    Not any more!
How old is she?
    Already, she's four!
She is growing up—
    (Well, that's a fact,
Even when stated
    With little tact).

At five, six, seven,
    The questions flow;
The same big people
    Still want to know:
Your age? Your weight?
    What is your name?
Where do you live?
    Each year the same.

One time I asked
    A dignified lady,
Who seemed surprised
    I was not a baby:
How old was she?
    How much she weighed?
She turned away
    And looked dismayed.

She answered not
    As I had done,
The same questions
    Since I was one.
Instead, she said
    It was unfair,
To ask her age,
    And weight, right there.

When will it stop,
    This silly game?
How old are you,
    And what's your name?
Adults don't know
    How to address,
Little folk they
    Try to impress.

MY HIDE-AWAY

I have a secret hide-away
    Back of the couch;
When Sister's friends come in to play,
    That's where I crouch.

To them I listen as they talk,
    Without a sound;
They think I've gone out for a walk
    But I'm around.

When of their dates they chance to speak,
    I hardly breathe;
Their inner secrets they may leak,
    For me to thieve.

Most often though I can't restrain
    Myself so well;
From laughter I do not refrain,
    Then they can tell—

That I've been listening so intent
    In my wee nook,
To all the stories they invent,
    Not in the book.

Discovered then, I run, you bet,
    Right out the door;
I wait 'til they that day forget,
    Then hide once more.

THE OCEAN WAVES

A great big ocean wave
    Jumped right on top of me,
And then it slapped my face
    For playing in the sea.

Another picked me up
    And threw me on the shore;
Then the waves shook their fists,
    And dared me come for more.

DISAPPOINTMENT

To Daddy's eyes comes that look again
    Each time he sees an electric train;
That he loves his daughters well we know,
    For much affection he does show;
But at Christmas time, and birthdays too,
    When he buys a new doll dressed in blue,
We suspect it would have brought him joy
    If one of his girls had been a boy.

BIG SISTER'S ROOM

Big Sister's room is an exciting place,
    It's filled with bottles and fancy lace;
Upon her shelves are lots of things,
    A shiny horse, and a bell that rings,
A tiny bottle, so bright and red,
    A beautiful doll with a broken head,
Powder and lipstick and sweet perfume—
    All this, and more, in Big Sister's Room.

During the day, while Big Sister's away,
  I slip to her room for fun and play;
The bottles I open, her clothes I wear,
  The sweet perfume I put on my hair;
Jewels, and hair pins, and shoes with heels,
  Make me a big lady with many appeals;
Books with pictures, a tiny whisk-broom—
  Are among the wonders in Big Sister's Room.

In Big Sister's Room, I'm not supposed to play,
  Mother keeps watch while Sister's away;
The door is kept shut, I cannot go near,
  This wonderful place with its treasures so dear.
Big Sister is sweet and to me is so good,
  She loves me I'm sure as a sister should;
But as for her room, while she is at school,
  "Stay out of my things," is always her rule.

SOMEONE TO WALK FOR ME

When I was sick and couldn't walk,
I took a piece of clay;
And made a child who couldn't talk,
But she could walk all day.

I stood her by my window bright,
Each morning as a rule;
She'd walk for me from morn 'til night,
While others were at school.

When I got well and walked again
I kissed my child of clay;
"You'll never know what help you've been,
To walk for me each day."

IN-BETWEEN YEARS

So eager to part the curtain of adult life;
Yet reluctant to walk on the stage of
responsibility

IN-BETWEEN

When I was twelve my wish supreme
    Was to be taken for thirteen;
The twelfth year is an in-between—
    You're not a child; nor yet a teen.

PARENTS!

My crazy, mixed-up parents,
    Anxious, confused and naïve;
About today's teen-agers,
    They know not what to believe.

CENTER OF ATTENTION

All eyes are on me
When I walk into the room;
My heart beats madly
With each rustle of my dress,
Awe and uncertainty
Reach out to greet me. . . .

Or so it seems at age thirteen.

SLUMBER PARTY

Ten girls on a slumber party,
  Loads of food and laughter hearty;
Candid pictures one could sell,
  And stories that we shouldn't tell.

The clock strikes twelve and still no sleep,
  When Mother comes there's not a peep;
At one o'clock still going strong,
  Ten happy girls break out in song.

Gruff growls from Father then commence
  And snickers break the strained suspense;
At two one scarcely hears a sound,
  At three the covers can't be found.

At five the night is almost gone—
  Yet the party stills goes on;
With gags and stunts and a pillow fight,
  The fun has lasted through the night.

When morning comes, ten sleepy girls
  Have heavy eyes and tangled curls;
No single one among their number,
  Through the night had any slumber.

HOW WILL I LOOK?

How will I look when I grow up?
    Will my hair be fair? My eyes blue?
Tall or short? How much will I weigh?
    My face, would I could picture, too.

Each year anew my features change,
    The final state I yearn to know;
Will I perchance look like my dad,
    Or more like Mother as I grow?

Perhaps I'll look a bit like both,
    With one's nose and the other's chin;
If such be true, I hope that I
    Have Mother's figure trim and thin.

My father's feet; Oh perish the chance!
    I'd be a sight; would nature dare?
His smile I'd take, perhaps his ears,
    His complexion, but not his hair.

Could I but choose between the two,
    The traits I'd most like to borrow;
Would I be content, I wonder,
    To mold myself for tomorrow?

WHO, ME?

What if there is much work to be done
　　To get ready to go to the city;
Isn't there a need for only one,
　　To just stand around and look pretty?

BARGAINING

What do I get
  For a good report?
Come on, now, Dad,
  Be a good sport.
I work real hard
  At school, don't I?
A little reward
  Will make me try
All the harder
  To do my best,
On daily work
  And six-weeks' test.
Beside I need
  Some extra funds;
My shoes are worn,
  My hose have runs.
I'm glad to study,
  As heaven knows,
When you'll buy me
  A few new clothes.

THE COVER-UP

That I don't care
    Is not quite true,
I just can't show
    The truth to you.

The best defense
    For one who's taunt,
Is to laugh and
    Be nonchalant.

FAMILY DECISIONS

When together we make plans for a trip,
    Some of the places we decide to skip
Hold interest for Mother, Sister and me—
    But Daddy's one vote counts more than our three.

TEEN-AGE FRIENDS

We are friends, yet—
    When boys are close
You sure can bet;

We compete, yes—
    And our friendship
At times grows less.

With boys not near,
    Again we hold
Each other dear.

We're normal, since—
    Both of us are
Ad - o - les - cents.

IN STYLE

Go cut my hair?
    I wouldn't dare:
I always wear
    It long. See there—
That girl, how short,
    But she's that sort.

Another girl,
    Hair all awhirl,
Her name is Pearl;
    But she's a churl!
She may not care
    What others wear.

There's Mary, too,
    With haircut new;
I wonder who—
    Oh, look, it's Sue.
Could it be wrong
    To wear hair long?

To wear a braid,
    And masquerade
The promenade
    In a parade—
It's not for me
    I now can see.

To be in chime,
    All of the time,
Is most sublime,
    Just like a rhyme.
My hair's in style—
    Now for awhile.

"THE" NIGHT

The time is near,
    Steps I'll soon hear;
Does what I wear
    Become my hair?
Be calm, Mother,
  Just take another
Look at my dress—
    This room's a mess!

Father don't tease
    Now if you please,
And wear your shoes
    Bare feet don't amuse;
Try to act right
    For this one night;
Straighten your tie,
    Do help, please try!

Was that a car?
    He can't be far;
I feel just fine
    But it's past nine;
Will he be late
    For my first date!
Oh! there's the bell,
    And all is well.

LOST VACATION

On a vacation
    There can be no joy,
When one does not meet
    A single new boy.

By a quirk of fate,
    We made a mistake;
We stayed a week on
    The wrong side the lake.

Across the water
    Was a big boys' camp;
Too far for swimming,
    Too distant to tramp.

No doubt my true love
    Was waiting me there;
Tall, dark and handsome,
    With smart, wavy hair.

But I won't lose hope,
    Continue to dream;
I still have some time—
    I'm only fourteen.

OLDERN TIMES

In oldern times my parents lived,
 They were young like me they say;
But they're old fashioned as can be,
 Out-of-step with life today.

Their ideas old do not quite fit
 New fashions and modern pace;
The world has changed, but they don't know
 How much they are out-of-place.

How glad am I that I was not
 Born in oldern times, so drear;
Contemporary I will be,
 So chic and stylish, my dear.

My children I will not embarrass
 With habits out of the past;
My only problem I can see—
 Will what's new today, just last?

Or will tomorrow's oldern times
 Be these I hold impassioned?
Should such be true, my children then,
 Might find me quite old fashioned.

A MOTHER'S REGRET

A mother's anxiety greatly grows,
  When she finds her daughter wearing her clothes;
When mother-and-daughter dresses are one,
  The rearing of daughter is too near done—
No greater regret to mother is known,
  Than comes when daughter is almost full-grown.

HOLD THE PHONE

Do other parents wonder as well,
    Whether Alexander Graham Bell,
If a teen-aged daughter he had known,
    Would have invented the telephone?

A PLEA TO FATHERS OF SONS

If power to live this life a man,
    A father would pass to his son,
Of all the lessons he must teach,
    Place greatest stress upon this one—

No one a gentleman is born,
    Such status he cannot inherit;
By how he lives each may aspire
    This title, justly, to merit.

For each in a democracy,
    Must by his own acts earn respect;
A man's a man for what he is,
    Not who he was in retrospect.

This lesson, fathers, teach your sons;
    And those of us who daughters rear,
Will not lose sleep whene'er they come
    On bended knee, a "yes" to hear.

FOR A HAPPY FAMILY

It's not the moods or moments,
With which a family's blest;
But what is done with each
That brings life at its best.

So catch each mood or moment,
It's flavor carefully keep;
Re-live it oft' with loved ones,
And happiness you'll reap.

ALMOST FULL GROWN

Reaching for Tomorrow

Assessment

Measure man by all dimensions,
By his deeds, his honor true;
Discount some of his good intentions—
An ounce of faith should count as two.

Belonging

Everyone yearns, above all, to belong
  To a group of close friends with loyalties strong;
Lucky is the one who has found a place,
  With people to serve and problems to face;
A life-time of joy waits for all to share
  With that rarest of souls who has learned to care;
Welcome are the ones who have heard this call,
  They win our hearts, and belong to us all.

Travel Guide

Life is not a perfect highway
With no bumps along each day;
Even when you travel "my" way,
All will not be bright and gay.

Shock absorbers will be needed
Is advice that best be heeded;
Such protection can't be deeded,
Is a fact to be conceded.

Build a faith that will sustain you,
With skies grey as well as blue;
Train your mind to cherish virtue,
And let each day be always new.

(To Judy—in her first year of college.)

Priority

The best should teach,
The next may preach,
Though some must heal the sick;
If I could say
To each his way,
This order I would pick.
All else is naught
Unless it's taught
With wisdom, skill and power;
The world awaits
The opening gates,
By teachers of the hour.

Feedback

It's the image of another
Be he foe, or be he brother,
Which I depict for all to see
That the public receives of me.

Empathy

Life is pretty much a mirror,
  Reflecting back just what we give;
If you do not like the image,
  Better change the way you live.

Curiosity

Ah, so tiny, and faint,
  almost imperceptible,
  is thy glow;
The smouldering, quaint,
  highly intellectual,
  will to know.

Obsolete

Soft, white jet streams
write an ancient message
across the sky:
Ever it seems,
modern is a moment,
and then must die.

Vanity

Man spends much time and
A great part of his labour,
Trying to prove that he's
Better than his neighbor.

Hate

Hate is a double-edged sword, pointed at both ends, without a handle; it cannot be raised against another without injury to the wielder.

Doubt

Doubt is a leak in the dyke of positive action; if left unplugged, it will grow into a rupture to drain one's reservoir of energy in a destructive, uncontrollable flood.

Dawn or Dusk

How can I know the difference
Between the sun's rise and its set?
Both appear in brilliant radiance;
They are almost alike, but yet—
The one brings in the bright new day,
With curling smoke and birds singing;
It awakens us to run and play
'til time to hear the school bells ringing.
The other, which seems much the same,
Soon fades from red to purple hue;
It pulls the night down all around,
Hangs out the stars and brings the dew.
If should I but mistake the two,
The sunset for the morning light,
I'd think the glow of dying day
The golden rays of new life bright.

Left Out

We played together as though one,
  Our childhood days were lots of fun;
Then circumstances came about,
  That some of us must get left out.

Like older folks we organize,
  And hardly do we realize
That when we vote for one or two,
  The one left out may well be you.

Though disappointments come your way,
  You'll live to see another day;
It's not a thing to cry about,
  If you're the one who gets left out.

Just do your part with all the rest,
  Help those elected to do their best;
Follow their lead, and be a good scout,
  And you'll forget that you were left out.

In play, in life, rules are the same,
  Keep your chin up, and play the game;
Do a good job, and there's no doubt,
  The time will come when you're not left out.

Seasoning

With beaded brow,
He stood there now,
With ball in hand to throw;
The crowd was tense
With strained suspense—
The outcome soon they'd know!

He knew the score,
T'was five to four,
With his team out in front;
Two men were out,
This one, about,
And one, safe on a bunt.

The last inning,
He dreamed of winning
This National Championship;
Two strikes he'd thrown
Well it was known,
Now by a third he'd slip.

The catcher called
For his fast ball,
It was his Sunday toss;
He let it go,
Real hard, just so,
And grooved it straight across.

With one movement,
The ball he sent,
And started off the field;
His work was done,
The game he'd won,
The championship was sealed.

A mighty cheer
Then reached his ear,
He'd be a great hero
They'd sing his praise
For days and days,
His fame would ever grow.

A loud, sharp crack
Brought his mind back
To the ball he just had thrown
It'd been hit square,
Was going fair
To parts, for it, unknown.

One home-run ball,
And that was all,
He'd lost, instead of won;
He was to blame,
His glory, shame—
What a terrible thing he'd done!

He wept because
The crowd's applause
Was for the other man;
There in a trance
He begged a chance
To throw that one again.

The dressing room
Was filled with gloom,
And then the coach spoke clear;
"Forget it now,
And anyhow,
We'll try again next year."

"Learn this one thing:
To take defeat's sting,
While playing Little League Ball.
From your mistake
This lesson take,
And it will ease your fall.

"In Legion Ball,
And Big Leagues, all,
The rule is just the same—
Don't groove your throw
Across, just so,
If you would win the game."

Secrets

If you have a secret,
  And you want it kept well;
Just give it to "no one"—
  "No one" can ever tell.

Of others' misfortune,
  You should happen to learn;
Don't tell a "single soul"—
  Though his ears fairly burn.

In all that you may say
  About what you have heard;
Avoid that big gossip,
  The well-known "little bird".

Others you dare not trust
  Are neighbors and "your friend";
Remember that each "some one",
  May well tell in the end.

If you're broken hearted,
  Just tell it to a few
Close friends and your family—
  They will know what to do.

If you have some good news,
  And you want all to know;
Don't you tell "any one"—
  On your face it will show.

Youth and Age

Two men, together, there now stand,
  A callow youth, an older man;
Each wishes that to some degree
  More like the other he could be.

The one craves wisdom, you might guess,
  The elder yearns for youthfulness;
They covet two traits seldom found
  In just one person to abound.

For nature has things so arranged
  Youth for wisdom must be exchanged;
Yet need they envy each and dream—
  Youth and age make a perfect team.

Round-Up Time

When the sun beats down,
  And winter is past;
When wild flowers bloom,
  Where the snow was last;
When animals shed
  Their warm furry coats;
Birds take special care
  In singing their notes;
When new cactus blooms
  Reach up toward the sky;
All are sure signs that
  Round-up time is nigh.

Coyotes wierd yelping
At night to their pups;
Bees buzzing merrily
'Round spring buttercups;
Lean rattlesnakes stalk
The prairie dog brown;
And cowboys ride from,
Instead toward, the town;
Calves are frisky and
Crickets are strumming—
Tell all the world the
Round-up is coming.

Ranch hands are busy
Oiling their leather;
The boss looks often
Out at the weather;
The chuck-wagon's wheels
Are given fresh grease;
Flying North is seen
A flock of Wild Geese—
Better pick your mount,
One you can climb,
And join with the boys
At Spring Round-up Time.

Cattle start trickling
From hills all around,
With cowboys scouring
Each patch of ground;
There in the distance
You see the dust rise;
They're strung out for miles
Right before your eyes;
Cow-punchers riding
The flanks and the points.
Whooping and hollering,
And stretching their joints.

They sing as they ride
And shout to the herds;
Their songs are made up
Of strange jingling words:
"Yippie, Ho! Move along,
Don't you stray, TI, YI!
The ones left behind
Most surely will die.
Hup, Hup, you critters,"
Thus goes the rhyme,
"You know why we're here—
It's your round-up time".

When evening shadows
  Turn green grass to brown
And all weary cows
  Have been bedded down;
You'll welcome the smell
  Of a camp-fire burning,
And fresh barbeque
  On the spit turning;
In the dutch-oven
  You'll find new-made bread
There's hot coffee, too,
  Before time for bed.

While not on night watch
  Your rest is complete
Snug in your bedroll
  You miss the hoofbeat
Of feeding horses,
  And a wandering cow,
Who'll try to slip through
  The night guard somehow.
You'll dream of cattle,
  The dreaded stampede
Of men riding hard
  With you in the lead.

In too few short hours
   To watch, it's your turn;
That you're not alone,
   You sure soon to learn;
To sooth resting stock
   You whistle a tune,
A night owl answers
   From out toward the moon;
And far in the distance
   A cougar will call—
They're helping you watch;
   Just don't sleep, that's all.

Long before daybreak
   You're moving along,
Riding a fresh horse
   And singing a song:
"Wake up, start moving,
   String out, Yippi Ti;
Go on to your round-up
   You can't pass it by".
Through rain, wind and dust,
   For day after day,
You ride to round-up
   In true Western Way.

When all are gathered
  In one big cow-herd,
The boss mounts his horse
  And then gives the word.
The strays are cut out,
  The doggies are fed,
And soon branding irons
  Are heated bright red;
Skilled cowboys with ropes
  Throw over-handed,
Then drag the new calves
  Out to be branded.

Each bellowing calf
  Is flanked on its side,
The hot branding iron
  Is touched to its hide.
Then his ear is marked,
  To make doubly sure,
From a maverick's lot
  He's always secure.
Each thoroughbred calf
  Will get a name, too,
Stamped in his ear by
  The process, Tattoo.

When all are branded,
  Counted and numbered,
And you wake to guess
  How long you've slumbered;
The herd is dispersed
  To grass meadow lands;
And back toward the town
  Ride all the cow-hands;
Horses are footloose,
  Turned out to clover—
With regret you know
  The round-up is over.

In dreams you'll re-live
  The whirl of a rope,
The sound of hoof-beats
  Of horses in lope;
The smell of leather
  And freshly burned hair;
And the cowboy's song,
  "Ti, Yi, Get in there".
You'll hear spurs jingle,
  With nature in chime,
As always they do
  At Spring Round-up Time.

Immortality

Said a stately Birch to the lark,
Just write your song on my bark,
That all may sing as they pass by;
As long as I stand, it won't die.

When I shall fall, I'll set it free,
For life it needn't depend on me;
The wind will take it far away,
Where others may sing again your lay.

Once recorded your song may live,
And to future ages pleasure give;
With my help you may possibly
Give to your words immortality.

A DEDICATED BOOK

Royalties from the original printing of *Moods and Moments* went to establish a scholarship for teachers of handicapped children at the University of Virginia. Income from this re-printing will go to support **THE BEST SHOULD TEACH** Funds at the University of Colorado at Boulder and the Fort Lewis College at Durango, Colorado.

These two institutions, the author's alma maters, have pledged to disseminate this social wisdom forever to future generations. Hence, for your purchase, you not only will share the excitement of the rhymes and rhythms and the probes to reflection of its poems you will be contributing to efforts to make teaching seen as the preeminent profession that nourishes all other professions and the total of human endeavors-the key to a better world

If you agree with this premise and wish to support further this effort, contributions can be sent to THE BEST SHOULD TEACH FUNDS at either or both of these institutions.

CU Foundation
The University of Colorado
P. O. Box 1140
Boulder, CO 80306

Fort Lewis Foundation
Fort Lewis College
1000 Rim Drive
Durango, CO 81301-3999

DR. LINDLEY J. STILES IN FRONT OF **THE BEST SHOULD TEACH** STATUE AT THE UNIVERSITY OF COLORADO

ABOUT THE AUTHOR:

Dr. Lindley J. Stiles is a rare multi-talented person. He is known world-wide for the 60 cutting-edge professional books he authored and/ or edited as well as over 400 articles that were read the world over. As the nation's outstanding Dean of Education at the Universities of Virginia and Wisconsin, he led a reform of the way teachers are trained in the U. S., and fathered the Funded Research Movement for improving education. His genius was recognized by Northwestern University when it appointed him the first Interdisciplinary Professor of Education in the World.

Then, a real rarity, he wrote prize-winning poetry for children and young people-a total of four books and many individual poems.His poetry is prized not only for its stimulating rhymes and rhythms but, most importantly, for the human values it emphasizes and its sensitivity to the reactions of readers to their life experiences.

Listed in over thirty Who's Who types of reference books, sixteen of which are dedicated to him, among others, he is a true world-class educator, writer, poet, and lecturer. The American Biographical Institute calls him one of the greatest minds of the 21th Century; The British International Biographical Centre has named him one of a few "Greatest Living Legends" for his career achievements and, particularly, his creation of the social wisdom **THE BEST SHOULD TEACH**.

Additional information about Dr. Stiles can be found in two web pages which are maintained for him:

www.internationalbiographicalcentre.com

thebestshouldteach.org

www.ingramcontent.com/pod-product-compliance
Ingram Content Group UK Ltd.
Pitfield, Milton Keynes, MK11 3LW, UK
UKHW040017200726
13854UKWH00001B/253

9 781412 008822